D

SKILLS JOURNAL

¿Amazing English!™

AN INTEGRATED ESL CURRICULUM

Michael Walker

Addison-Wesley Publishing Company

A Publication of the World Language Division

Director of Product Development: Judith M. Bittinger
Executive Editor: Elinor Chamas
Editorial Development: Kathleen M. Smith, Peggy T. Alper
Text and Cover Design: Taurins Design Associates
Art Direction and Production: Taurins Design Associates
Production and Manufacturing: James W. Gibbons

Illustrators: Teresa Anderko 4, 99; Delores Bego 14; Susan Lexa 9, 13, 22, 26, 62; Karen Loccisano 12, 66, 80, 84; Frank Mayo 8, 76, 102; Susan Miller 23, 27, 40, 41, 48, 49, 61, 68, 69, 82; Karen Schmidt 32, 79; Nina Wallace 5.

ISBN 0-201-85378-7

3 4 5 6 7 8 9 10-CRS-99 98 97

CONTENTS

A. Write your ideas and thoughts about the unit theme, "We Work and Play." What do you think the unit will be about? What do you and your friends like to do in your free time? What work do you want to do when you are older?

_____

_____

_____

_____

_____

_____

_____

_____

B. As you go through the unit, write your thoughts about each page. What would you like to find out more about? Use extra paper if you need more space.

_____

_____

_____

_____

_____

_____

_____

_____

_____

(Supports Student Book D, page 3) **Prewriting; predicting.** In Exercise A, students write their thoughts after participating in the class discussion of the unit opener page. Encourage students to come back to this page periodically to complete Exercise B. You may want to save this page in the student's **Assessment Portfolio.**

C. Use the notes and ideas you wrote on page 2 to write about "We Work and Play." What did you like most in the unit? Why? What did you like least? Why? What did you learn?

_____

_____

_____

_____

_____

_____

_____

_____

_____

_____

_____

_____

_____

_____

_____

_____

_____

(Supports Student Book D, Theme 1. Use after page 22.) **Writing opinions; using notes; recalling details; summarizing; self-assessment.** This page provides an opportunity for students to sum up their thoughts about the unit and to tell what they learned. You may want to save this page in the student's **Assessment Portfolio**.

A. *Look at the map below and answer the questions. Use the words in the Data Bank to find the places.*

DATA BANK

1. city	2. town	3. forest	4. river
5. lake	6. coast	7. mountains	8. desert

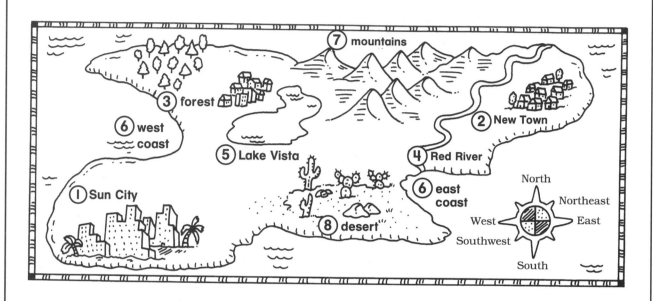

1. Is Sun City in the northeast or in the southwest? *in the southwest*

2. Is the forest by the west coast or by the east coast? _____

3. Is New Town by a lake or by a river? _____

4. Is the desert in the north or in the south? _____

5. Where are the mountains? _____

B. *Now answer these questions.*

1. Where is your city or town? _____

2. Do you live in a small, large, or medium-sized community? _____

(Supports Student Book D, page 4) **Home-School Connection; vocabulary development; map reading.**
Students find places on map. Then discuss the location of your city or town. Accept short answers. Students can also talk about locations of their native cities, towns, and villages. Have students take this page home to share with their families.

PROBLEM **S**OLVING

Sports Day

The boys and girls from Skunk, Rocky City, and Fish schools are having a sports day. They are competing in several events. Below is the scoreboard. The winner of each event gets four points. The team in second place gets two points. The team in third place gets one point (for effort!).

	Event	Skunk	Rocky	Fish
	Relay race	4	2	1
	High jump	1	4	2
	50-yard dash	1	2	4
	Long jump	2	4	1
	3-legged race	4	1	2

Look at the chart below. Fill in the missing information about the teams in the school competition.

	First	Second	Third
Relay race	Skunk	Rocky	Fish
High jump	Rocky	_____	_____
50-yard dash	_____	_____	_____
Long jump	_____	_____	_____
3-legged race	_____	_____	_____

(Supports Student Book D, page 5) **Solving problems logically; identifying people, places, and actions; interpreting/completing a chart.** Students will enjoy filling in the chart. They can compare answers and discuss school competitions. Ask them how many points each team earned and which teams won the most events.

A. *Did you enjoy making a math slat book? Read about China, yesterday and today. Then answer the questions.*

More than 3,000 years ago, people in ancient China carved writing on pieces of bone and tortoiseshell. The Chinese alphabet is made up of pictographs, or picture letters. These are called **characters.** For example, the character that means "field" is a square divided into four parts.

If you went to China, you could see a huge wall made of stone, earth, and brick. It's called the Great Wall, and it was built about 2,300 years ago to protect the Chinese people from invaders. The wall is 1,500 miles (2,414 kilometers) long, and it took more than 300,000 workers to build it!

More than 1 **billion** people live in China today. That means about 21 percent of the people in the whole world live there. Also, China has one of the world's youngest populations—75 percent of its citizens are younger than 35 years old.

1. What are the letters of the Chinese alphabet called?

_____

2. How are they different from the letters of the English alphabet?

_____

3. Why was the Great Wall built?

_____

4. How many miles long is it?

_____

5. About how many people live in China today?

_____

6. Is the population of China made up of mostly older or mostly younger people?

_____

B. *Find out more about the Chinese calendar. Write your information on a separate piece of paper.*

(Supports Student Book D, page 6) **Reading for a purpose; research; note-taking.** Correct Exercise A in class. Accept long or short answers. You may want to assign Exercise B as small-group work. You may want to save this page in the student's **Assessment Portfolio.**

The Boy Who Cried Wolf

A. *Answer the questions about the story on student page 7.*

1. What was the boy watching? _____

2. What did he cry out? _____

3. Who came running to help? _____

4. What did the people do? _____

5. How many times did the boy cry wolf? _____

6. What happened when there really
   was a wolf? _____

B. *First, write the missing letters to complete the words. Then find
   and circle the words in the puzzle. Which two words are in the
   puzzle twice?*

SH __ __ __ __ RD   VI __ __ __ __ ER   L __ __ T   L __ __ __ S

H __ __ P   AT __ __ __ K   SH __ __ P   TR __ __ __

REA __ __ __   F __ __ L   W __ __ F   __ __ OCK   __ __ KE

S	H	E	P	H	E	R	D	T	U	S	R
H	F	P	A	M	D	E	I	F	G	N	Z
E	T	T	R	O	L	A	T	T	A	C	K
E	B	F	C	V	I	L	L	A	G	E	R
P	N	L	Q	W	A	L	O	T	M	H	D
L	W	O	L	F	R	Y	S	R	S	C	W
O	M	C	X	O	S	D	T	U	L	T	I
S	U	K	J	O	K	E	B	T	T	V	X
T	R	E	A	L	L	Y	U	H	E	L	P

(Supports Student Book D, page 7) **Reading for a purpose; word search.** Accept short answers for Exercise
A. You may want to assign Exercise B as pairwork.

7

A

1. Do you ride a bike or a horse?   *I ride a bike.*

2. Do they play baseball or tennis?

3. Does she eat apples or oranges
   for lunch?

1. What do they watch after school?   *They watch TV.*

2. What does she wash every month?

3. What does he brush every day?

 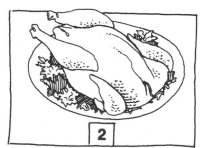 

1. What does it say?   *It says "Hi!"*

2. What do they eat on Thursdays?

3. What does she often read?

(Supports Student Book D, pages 8-9) **Identifying habitual actions; using third person present tense.** Go over examples in each section before students write answers. Pay special attention to final -s/-es endings.

| I | 2 | 3 |

1. What does it always bury in the yard? _____

2. What does she dry in the morning? _____

3. Where do they hurry to every day? _____

| I | 2 | 3 |

1. What does he usually buy for a snack? _____

2. What does she carry to school? _____

3. What do they play? _____

  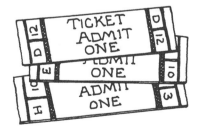

| I | 2 | 3 |

1. What do they like? _____

2. What does he fix? _____

3. What does she need? _____

(Supports Student Book D, pages 8-9) **Identifying habitual actions; using third person present tense.**
Review final -s/-es endings, and -y to -ies on student page 8 before students write answers.

9

A. *Match the words with their definitions. Write the correct letter on the line. You may need to use a dictionary.*

1. shallow ____   a. movable, easy to carry

2. prototype ____   b. the opposite of **deep**

3. terrain ____   c. to make or process

4. release ____   d. type of land, such as desert or mountain

5. portable ____   e. model or example for making something new

6. manufacture ____   f. to let go

B. *Look at the chart and answer the questions.*

Inventor	Invention	Country
Alexander Graham Bell	Telephone	United States
Galileo	Thermometer	Italy
Thomas Edison	Phonograph	United States
Wilhelm Roentgen	X-ray	Germany
Clarence Birdseye	Frozen Food	United States

1. Who invented frozen food?   _____

2. What country did the inventor of the X-ray live in?   _____

3. What did Galileo invent?   _____

4. What country was Edison from?   _____

5. What did Bell invent?   _____

(Supports Student Book D, pages 10-11) **Vocabulary development; using a dictionary; reading /interpreting a chart.** Students can complete Exercise A independently and exchange papers to correct. Check answers to Exercise B with whole class.

C. *Invent a vehicle of your own. What will it look like? How many wheels will it have? How fast will it go? Who will use it? Where will it be used? Will it be used for fun or for work? Describe your vehicle, and then draw a picture of it.*

_____

_____

_____

_____

_____

_____

_____

_____

_____

(Supports Student Book D, page 11) **Vocabulary development; organizational planning; creative writing.**
Be sure to discuss the writing-prompt questions thoroughly before assigning. Students can complete the exercise individually, with a partner, or in a small group. You may want to save this page in the student's
Assessment Portfolio.

A Solve the problems, as in the example.

Example: He can't lift this box.   *Ben can help him.*

1. She can't open the door.   _____

2. They can't read.   _____

3. We can't start our car.   _____

4. I can't close the window.   _____

Write what you hope, as in the example .

Example: They have a snake.   *I hope they bring it with them.*

1. She has a gorilla.   _____

2. He has a kangaroo.   _____

3. We have a mouse.   _____

4. I have a dog.   _____

Answer the questions, as in the example.

Example: Where is Andres?   *I can see him.*
    He is behind the swing.

1. Where is Gila?   _____

      _____

2. Where are the boys?   _____

      _____

(Supports Student Book D, pages 12-13) **Object pronouns.** Go over examples with students. The third exercise includes review of prepositions. Answers to number 2 will vary ("in the house; "in the tree"). Teach the word *treehouse.*

B *Look at the picture. Then answer the questions, as in the example.*

Example: What can they see in the mirror?   *They can see themselves.*

1. What can he see?   _____

2. What can she see?   _____

3. What can the dog see?   _____

Solve the problems, as in the example.

Example: Please help Carlos lift the box.   *Can't he do it himself?*

1. Please help Saeko wash the car.   _____

2. Please help the Scotts plant the trees.   _____

3. Please help us to paint the garage.   _____

4. Please help me do my homework.   _____

Write what happened, as in the example.

Example: What's the matter with her?   *She hurt herself.*

1. What's the matter with them?   _____

2. What's the matter with the cat?   _____

3. What's the matter with him?   _____

4. What's the matter with you?   _____

(Supports Student Book D, pages 12-13) **Reflexive pronouns.** Go over examples with class. Help students with pronoun changes (from *us* and *me* to *you* in the second exercise, numbers 3 and 4; from *you* to *I* in the third exercise, number 4).

Look at the map. Find the Mississippi River, and answer the questions.

1. What state is Lake Itasca in?

_____

2. Find the Gulf of Mexico, where the Mississippi River ends. What major city is located there?

_____

3. *Circle* **True** *or* **False:** Chicago, Illinois, is north of Indianapolis, Indiana.

4. Name three states that the Mississippi River flows through.

_____

_____

_____

5. *Circle* **True** *or* **False:** The Missouri River meets the Mississippi River at St. Louis, Missouri.

(Supports Student Book D, page 14) **Map reading; U.S. geography.** Be sure students can find the Mississippi River before assigning page. Students can work in pairs to complete exercise. Correct in class. Extension: Point out Hannibal, Mo.; explain who Mark Twain is. You may want to save this page in the student's **Assessment Portfolio.**

THEMEWORK **T**EAMWORK

Look at a detailed map of the United States, and answer the questions.

1. What are the names of the Great Lakes? What states do they border?

_____

_____

_____

_____

2. What is the highest mountain in the United States? Which state is it in?

_____

3. Which states border Canada?

_____

4. Which states border Mexico?

_____

_____

5. Santa Fe is the capital of _____.

6. Austin is the capital of _____.

(Supports Student Book D, page 15) **U.S. geography; research; note-taking; map reading.** Have students work in pairs. Suggest appropriate reference materials in addition to map of U.S. Accept long or short answers. Correct in class.

Liu-Always-In-A-Hurry

Try to answer the questions without looking at your student book. Then, use your student book to find the answers you're not sure about.

1. Where did the story take place?

_____

2. What was the farmer's name?

_____

3. Was the farmer patient or impatient? How do you know?

_____

4. Did the farmer worry about being careful?

_____

5. Who said, "My rice is already three inches high"?

_____

6. Where did Liu hurry to?

_____

7. What did Liu do then?

_____

8. How high were Liu's rice plants?

_____

9. What did he do to the plants?

_____

10. What happened to Liu's rice plants? Why?

_____

11. What did the people in the village say?

_____

12. What does "Don't be a rice puller!" mean?

_____

© Addison-Wesley Publishing Company

(Supports Student Book D, pages 16-19) **Understanding details in a story; understanding cause and effect; understanding sequence; making inferences.** Accept long or short answers. Correct with whole class. Students can write about/illustrate what they think Liu will do next.

Liu-Always-In-A-Hurry

Put the events in the story, "Liu-Always-In-A-Hurry," in the correct order. Number them 1 to 14. Then copy them on a separate piece of paper. Now you have told the story yourself—amazing! The first one is done for you.

____ Liu was always in a hurry.

____ One day, Lui was in the village.

____ He measured his rice.

_1_ Long ago, there lived a farmer named Liu.

____ Liu hurried home.

____ The people of the village heard about Liu's rice.

____ He rushed through everything.

____ He pulled each plant up until it was over three inches high.

____ The people in the village called Liu foolish.

____ People say, "Don't be a rice puller!"

____ He heard a farmer say that his rice was three inches high.

____ The next morning, he hurried out to his rice field.

____ "Now my rice is higher than anyone's," said Liu.

____ The little rice plants were dead.

© Addison-Wesley Publishing Company

(Supports Student Book D, pages 16-19) **Identifying sequence in a story; understanding details in a story**. Students complete the exercise independently. Correct as a class. Students can find other stories to rewrite out of sequence; then they can challenge each other to put the sentences in the correct order.

George Washington Carver

Use the words in the Data Bank. Finish the paragraphs about
George Washington Carver.

George Washington Carver was born in _____. His _____ was a

slave, so George was a _____, too. Slavery is _____ the law in the

United States today.

_____ the Civil War, slaves became free. George could have left the

Carver farm. But he didn't. Moses Carver's wife _____ him to read and

write.

When George was _____ years old, he _____ to school for the

first time. He _____ knew how to do many things. But he _____ to

learn more.

School was _____ free. George worked hard _____ earn the

money to pay for his education. And he _____ hard. He went to college

and studied _____. After graduation, he worked for the _____.

DATA BANK

wanted	not	against
already	fourteen	taught
studied	to	went
college	After	agriculture
Missouri	mother	slave

(Supports Student Book D, page 20) **Reading comprehension; cloze exercise; syntax.** Students read sentences from the story they listened to on student book page 20. This exercise provides an opportunity for students to review the story and to learn syntax. Correct in class. You may want to save this page in the student's **Assessment Portfolio**.

Make an Amazing Facts game of your own. Use facts from this book and your student book. You can write new facts, too. Write your questions in the squares. Write the correct answers on a separate piece of paper. Ask your teacher to check your game before you exchange games and play with friends.

(Supports Student Book D, page 22) **Creating a game; research; note-taking; socializing.** Encourage students to research answers they don't know. Store games in a box students can access during free time.

A. Write your ideas and thoughts about the unit theme, "Family Memories." What do you think the unit will be about? What kinds of activities does your family enjoy doing together? If you could visit a family living in another country, which country would you choose? Why?

_____

_____

_____

_____

_____

_____

_____

_____

B. As you go through the unit, write your thoughts about each page. What would you like to find out more about? Use extra paper if you need more space.

_____

_____

_____

_____

_____

_____

_____

_____

_____

(Supports Student Book D, page 23) **Home-School Connection; prewriting; predicting.** In Exercise A, students write their thoughts after participating in the class discussion of the unit opener page. Encourage students to come back to this page periodically to complete Exercise B. You may want to save a copy of this page in the student's **Assessment Portfolio.** Have students take this page home to share with their families.

C. Use the notes and ideas you wrote on page 20 to write about
   "Family Memories." What did you like most in the unit? Why?
   What did you like least? Why? What did you learn?

_____

_____

_____

_____

_____

_____

_____

_____

_____

_____

_____

_____

_____

_____

_____

_____

_____

(Supports Student Book D, Theme 2. Use after page 44.) **Home-School Connection; writing opinions; using notes; recalling details; summarizing; self-assessment.** This page provides an opportunity for students to sum up their thoughts about the unit and to tell what they learned. You may want to save a copy of this page in the student's **Assessment Portfolio**. Have students take this page home to share with their families.

A. *Circle the letter of the best response.*

1. How are you today?

    a. I'm glad to hear that.
    b. I'm not so good.
    c. I'm sorry to hear that.

2. What's the matter?

    a. Awful!
    b. Glad to hear that!
    c. I've got a headache.

3. I hope you feel better soon.

    a. Thanks. So do I.
    b. How about you?
    c. I'm sorry to hear that.

B. *Read carefully and complete the conversation.*

How are you today?   *Fine, thanks.* _____

I'm glad to hear that.   _____

I'm not so good.   _____

I have a cold.   _____

Thank you. So do I.   _____

C. *Who said what? Write the letters of the right pictures after the sentences.*

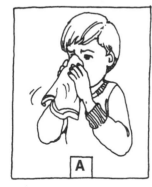   

1. I have an earache. _____

2. I have a broken arm. _____

3. I feel great! _____

4. I have a cold. _____

(Supports Student Book D, page 24) **Understanding sequence in conversations; creating dialogues from cues; describing health.** After students complete the exercises individually, check them together in class. You might want to do Exercise B with them to help them understand the format. Remind them to punctuate properly in Exercise B. Use Exercises A and B for dialogue practice.

PROBLEM SOLVING

Read about the Timmons's family day and answer the questions.
You may look at a clock while you solve the problem. (Hint: a
quarter to one is the same as 12:45.)

The Timmons family is going ice skating on Saturday. They can
walk to the skating rink from their house. The family includes
Mr. and Mrs. Timmons and their three children, Mandy, Sandy,
and Randy.

Mr. Timmons will arrive at the rink a half hour **after** Mrs.
Timmons. Mrs. Timmons is planning to arrive **with** Mandy.
Sandy will be there 15 minutes **before** Mr. Timmons. Randy will
arrive 10 minutes **before** Mandy. Mandy will be there at a
quarter to one.

1. Who will arrive at the skating rink first? _____.

2. Who is arriving at a quarter past one? _____.

3. How many minutes will Randy have to wait for Sandy to arrive?

_____.

4. Is Mandy arriving before or after Sandy? _____.

5. Who will arrive at the skating rink last? _____.

(Supports Student Book D, page 25) **Solving problems logically; analyzing clues; telling time.** Review
telling time with students before assigning this page. You may want to have students work in pairs. Correct in
class.

A. *The Huichol Indians are one Indian culture in Mexico.*
Another culture, from centuries ago, was the Mayan Indians.
Read about the Mayas, and then answer the questions.

The Mayas lived in Mexico, Guatemala, and Belize. Mayan
civilization was most developed from the years 300 to 900.
The Mayas had a calendar and a system of writing. They were
great mathematicians and astronomers. The first people to
have the idea of **zero** in math, the Mayas also figured out the
length of a solar year.

Today, you can see wonderful Mayan ruins. These include
huge ball courts, which the Mayas built to play their very
serious ball game. The game was played with a large rubber
ball. The players couldn't touch the ball with their hands or
feet, so they tried to hit it with their hips, elbows, or knees.
They had to cover those body parts with heavy padding. In
Mexico today, people still play a form of the Mayan ball game.

1. *Circle* **True** *or* **False:** Mayan civilization was most developed
   from the years 300 to 900.

2. *Fill in the blanks:* The Mayas invented the idea of _____ in math
   and figured out the length of the _____ year.

3. What kind of ball did the Mayas use in their ball game?

   _____

4. In the Mayan ball game, what parts of the body could the
   players use to hit the ball?

   _____

5. *Circle* **True** *or* **False:** In Mexico today, no one plays a ball game
   like the Mayan game.

B. *Find out about a modern Mexican ball game called* **jai a lai.** *On*
a separate piece of paper, write three amazing facts about it.

(Supports Student Book D, page 26) **Reading for a purpose; research; note-taking.** Correct in class. For
Exercise A, accept long or short answers. Show Mexico, Guatemala, and Belize on a map. Explain *solar year.*

Poetry Fun

Write the words from the Data Bank under the correct heading. Perhaps some words remind you of both winter and summer. Add words of your own, too. Then write a short poem. You may decide to have the poem rhyme or not. It's up to you.

DATA BANK

snow	sun	baseball	pool	ice	sleet
cold	sea	picnic	skate	hot	ice cream
lemonade	ski	snowflakes	shorts	shade	mittens
sail	swim	sled	dive	flowers	

Winter Words   **Summer Words**

_____ _____   _____ _____

_____ _____   _____ _____

_____ _____   _____ _____

_____ _____   _____ _____

_____ _____   _____ _____

_____ _____   _____ _____

_____ _____   _____ _____

_____

_____

_____

_____

_____

_____

(Supports Student Book D, page 27) **Classifying words; creative writing**. Encourage students to think about the images words evoke and then to write a rhyming or free-verse poem that they can share with the class. You may want to save this page in the student's **Assessment Portfolio**.

A Use the pictures to answer the questions.

MIKE | BROTHER | Example | SISTER

Example: Mike is thin.
What about his brother and sister?

His brother is thinner.
His sister is the thinnest.

MOTHER | FATHER | MARÍA | 1

1. María is tall.
What about her mother and father?

_____

_____

MRS. KING'S | MISS BLUME'S | MR. WONG'S | 2

2. Mr. Wong's car is old.
What about Mrs. King's car and Miss Blume's car?

_____

_____

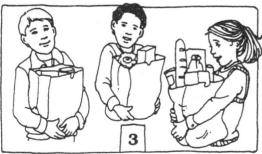

3

3. My bag is heavy.
What about Pedro's bag and Sara's bag?

_____

_____

A | B | C | 4

4. Baby A is sad.
What about Baby B and Baby C?

_____

_____

(Supports Student Book D, pages 28-29) **Comparatives and superlatives; matching written language with pictures.** Go over example with class, and then have students decide comparatives and superlatives based on pictures. Correct in class.

Answer the questions. Use complete sentences.

1. Larry's homework is difficult.
   What can you say about Jessica's homework and Ali's homework?

   Jessica's is more difficult.
   Ali's is the most difficult.

2. Melissa is a good swimmer.
   What can you say about her dog and her fish?

   _____

   _____

3. Josh is a bad dancer.
   What can you say about his mother and his father?

   _____

   _____

4. Caracas is an exciting city.
   What can you say about Tokyo and New York?

   _____

   _____

Now make up some comparisons, using the words given.

1. *boring* _____

   _____

   _____

2. *popular* _____

   _____

   _____

(Supports Student Book D, pages 28-29) **Comparatives and superlatives**. After students complete the exercises, they can exchange papers for correction. The class might want to create further comparisons based on their families, etc.

A. *Take a survey. Find out about family routines at your friends'
houses. Ask about one day. It can be a weekday or a weekend
day. Then fill in the chart.*

FAMILY ROUTINES	Name	Time Get Up	Time Go to Bed	Chores	Time Eat Dinner	Hours of TV Watching

(Supports Student Book D, page 30) **Home-School Connection; data collection; classifying; conducting a
survey; using a chart to record information; socializing; asking for/giving information; comparing and
contrasting.** After students fill in charts, they can report their findings to the class. Have students take this
page home to share with their families.

B. *Match the words with their definitions. Write the correct letter*
on the line. You may need to use a dictionary.

1. degree _____   a. exactly alike

2. wreck _____   b. sudden, strong rush of wind

3. gust _____   c. to hit or strike hard

4. identical _____   d. a unit on a scale showing temperature

5. flip _____   e. to throw in the air

6. knock _____   f. to destroy

C. *What if you could make your own rules? What would they be?*
Write some "house rules" for your family. Tell who in your
family would like your "rules" and who would not like them.
Give reasons for their opinions.

_____

_____

_____

_____

_____

_____

_____

_____

_____

_____

_____

_____

_____

(Supports Student Book D, pages 30-31) **Home-School Connection; vocabulary development; using the**
dictionary; creative writing; organizational planning. Have students complete Exercise B independently or
in pairs; correct in class. Before assigning Exercise C, brainstorm some possible "house rules" with the class.
Have students take this page home to share with their families.

Answer the questions about the story on student page 32.

1. What kind of a day was it? _____

2. What did the officer hear? _____

3. Where did she run? _____

4. What did the man have? _____

5. What did the officer see the
   next day? _____

6. Where was the man taking the
   lion the next day? _____

Underline the correct form of the verb.

1. She (hear, hears) a scream.

2. He (run, runs) in the park every day.

3. They (see, sees) lions at the zoo.

4. I (take, takes) the train to work.

5. You always (bring, brings) your dog with you.

6. We often (stand, stands) in line to get movie tickets.

Fill in the blanks with **do, does,** *or* **did**. *Be careful!*

1. I _____ not go to school every day. I go to school from Monday
   to Friday.

2. She _____ not ride to school. She walks.

3. They _____ not stand in line. They sit and wait instead.

4. I'm sorry. I _____ not hear what you said.

5. She _____ not drive a truck. She drove a bus.

6. They _____ not bring their cat. They brought their dog.

7. The officer _____ not tell me to wait. He told me to go home.

(Supports Student Book D, pages 32-33) **Reading for a purpose; irregular verbs.** Students work independently. Warn students to read both sentences before filling in the blanks in the third exercise. Correct in class. The first two exercises can be used for dialogue practice.

Fill in the blanks with **Do, Does,** *or* **Did.**

1. ★ _____ you bring your book with you?
   ● No, I brought my notebook. I forgot my book.

2. ★ _____ he drive a bus?
   ● No, he drives a truck.

3. ★ _____ he tell you to go?
   ● No, he told me to wait.

4. ★ _____ they run every day?
   ● No, they run only on Sundays.

5. ★ _____ you hear a scream?
   ● No, I didn't.

6. ★ _____ she tell your sister bedtime stories?
   ● Yes, she does. Every night.

7. ★ _____ they take milk and sugar?
   ● No, they take only milk.

Underline the correct form of the verb.

1. Do you (see, sees, saw) what I see?

2. Did they (bring, brings, brought) you a present?

3. Did she (drive, drives, drove) the truck yesterday?

4. Does he always (come, comes, came) home at nine?

5. Did she (feel, feels, felt) okay at the party?

6. Do we (go, goes, went) left or right at the corner?

7. Do you ever (tell, tells, told) lies?

8. Did they (stand, stands, stood) in line all day?

9. Did he (eat, eats, ate) before the show?

(Supports Student Book D, page 33) **Reading for a purpose; irregular verbs.** Students work independently. Warn students to read both sentences before filling in the blanks in the first exercise. Correct in class. The first exercise can be used for dialogue practice.

Read the article and answer the questions.

Captain James Cook, the English explorer, sailed in the Pacific Ocean. In 1770, he explored the east coast of what is now Australia. He asked the natives about the strangest animal he had ever seen. The natives said, "Kangaroo!" That means, more or less, "It would be hopeless to try to tell you."

Kangaroos still fascinate us today. They are members of the marsupial family. That means they are mammals with pouches. Kangaroos are vegetarians. They don't eat other animals. And kangaroo babies are tiny when they are born. A newborn kangaroo is less than one inch long! It finds its way to its mother's pouch and lives there for many months.

Kangaroos love to box. A kangaroo's hands are very much like a human's hands. A kangaroo "puts its fists up," holding them close to its chest. Then it jabs and hops and punches, just like a boxer.

1. What continent did Captain Cook explore in 1770?

_____

2. What family of animals does the kangaroo belong to?

_____

3. What is special about marsupials?

_____

4. How big is a newborn kangaroo?

_____

5. Where does a baby kangaroo live during the first months of its life?

_____

6. Why does a kangaroo sometimes look like a boxer?

_____

(Supports Student Book D, page 34) **Reading for a purpose.** Accept long or short answers. Students can role-play answers in a "kangaroo-expert interview" and in the process correct their own work. You may want to save this page in the student's **Assessment Portfolio**.

Fill in the chart about famous explorers. Then choose one of the explorers to write more about on a separate piece of paper. Use the information you wrote on the chart to help you get started.

Explorer	Country Born In	Places Explored	Years Explored	Most Important Explorations
Vasco Núñez de Balboa				
Juan Ponce de León				
Ferdinand Magellan				

© Addison-Wesley Publishing Company

(Supports Student Book D, page 35) **Research; note-taking; data collection; using a chart to record information; comparing and contrasting; studying explorations.** Students may complete charts individually or in pairs. Go over completed charts with whole class. You may want to save this page in the student's **Assessment Portfolio**.

Family Pictures

*Open your student book to **Family Pictures**. Fill in the blanks or write your answers on the lines. Use the page numbers on the left to help you find the information.*

Page 36   1. Carmen Lomas Garza, the author of *Family Pictures*, writes

about growing up in _____.

Page 37   2. In the picture, the man wearing overalls and a blue shirt is

Carmen's _____.

3. Carmen is standing next to her _____

and her _____.

Page 38   4. Where is the family in this story? _____.

5. What are they eating? _____.

Page 39   6. Grandmother made a _____ out of her

_____.

7. Where is Carmen's brother? _____.

What is he doing? _____.

Page 40   8. Where was the fair held? _____. How

long did it last? _____.

9. What are the people in the picture buying and eating?

_____.

Page 41   10. Cakewalk is a _____ to raise

_____ to send Mexican Americans to the

_____.

(Supports Student Book D, pages 36-41) **Completing a cloze exercise; matching written language to pictures; identifying details in a story; finding specific information.** Make sure students know how to use student book for reference. Point out the two-part questions (numbers 7 and 8).

Family Pictures

Do you have a favorite family time? What is it like? Who participates? What does everyone do? Draw a picture of a special family time at your house. Then write about it.

(Supports Student Book D, pages 36-41) **Home-School Connection; creative writing; organizational planning; expressing ideas through art; expressing feelings.** Students can share their pictures and stories with whole class; you may want to post students' work on class bulletin board. You may want to save a copy of this page in the student's **Assessment Portfolio**. Have students take this page home to share with their families.

Robinson Family Adventure

Use the words in the Data Bank. Finish the paragraphs about the Robinson family's adventure.

My family and I were on a long trip. A _____ blew up, and our ship began _____ sink. The _____ left the ship in the lifeboats. They _____ us. The storm _____. We were _____ on the ship. But the ship was half sunk. We were shipwrecked at sea. The ship was half sunk on _____ rocks near _____ island. We searched the ship for _____. We _____ the wood and barrels. We _____ a boat and headed for the island.

The island was beautiful. We found _____ of good food. We found coconuts, sugar cane, wild potatoes, and _____. My wife _____ a little hill. _____ top of the hill, she found some huge, tall trees. We built a house in the trees.

DATA BANK

On	plenty	stopped
to	climbed	still
some	crew	supplies
an	found	built
storm	forgot	pineapple

(Supports Student Book D, page 42) **Reading comprehension; cloze exercise; syntax.** Students read sentences from the story they listened to on student book page 42. This exercise provides an opportunity for students to review the story and to learn syntax. Correct in class. You may want to save this page in the student's **Assessment Portfolio.**

Make an Amazing Facts game of your own. Use facts from this book and your student book. Write your questions in the squares. Write the correct answers on a separate piece of paper. Ask your teacher to check your game before you exchange games and play with friends.

(Supports Student Book D, page 44) **Creating a game; research; note-taking; socializing.** Encourage students to research answers they don't know. Store games in a box students can access during free time.

A. Write your ideas and thoughts about the unit theme, "That's Amazing!" What do you think the unit will be about? What amazing things do you know about? Have you had some amazing experiences in your life?

_____

_____

_____

_____

_____

_____

_____

_____

_____

_____

B. As you go through this unit, write your thoughts about each page. What would you like to find out more about? Use extra paper if you need more space.

_____

_____

_____

_____

_____

_____

_____

_____

(Supports Student Book D, page 45) **Prewriting; predicting.** In Exercise A, students write their thoughts after participating in the class discussion of the unit opener page. Encourage students to come back to this page periodically to complete Exercise B. You may want to save this page in the student's **Assessment Portfolio**.

C. Use the notes and ideas you wrote on page 38 to write about
"That's Amazing!" What did you like most in the unit? Why?
What did you like least? Why? What did you learn?

_____

_____

_____

_____

_____

_____

_____

_____

_____

_____

_____

_____

_____

_____

_____

_____

_____

_____

_____

_____

(Supports Student Book D, Theme 3. Use after page 66.) **Writing opinions; using notes; recalling details; summarizing; self-assessment.** This page provides an opportunity for students to sum up their thoughts about the unit and to tell what they learned. You may want to save this page in the student's **Assessment Portfolio**.

Fill in the blanks to make a telephone conversation.

Hello?

_____. Is _____ there? This is _____.

I'm _____, _____. _____ is not here.

Will you ask him to call _____?

Certainly. What's your _____?

My telephone number is _____. Please ask _____ to call me before _____.

Call _____ before _____. Is that your message?

Yes, that's my _____.

Okay, _____. I'll give _____ your message.

_____. Good-bye.

_____, _____.

(Supports Student Book D, page 46) **Role-playing fixed and free dialogues; creating new dialogues from cues; socializing.** Have students role-play the telephone conversation, filling in blanks with appropriate responses. Then have them work in pairs or groups to make up their own phone dialogues.

PROBLEM SOLVING

A. *Pecos Bill was an amazing cowboy! Solve these problems about Bill's fantastic feats.*

1. Pecos Bill could rope more cows than anyone else! Every time Bill threw his lasso, he roped 5 cows. On Friday, Bill threw his lasso 4 times. How many cows did he rope that day?

2. Pecos Bill was the best cow herder who ever lived. On Monday, he herded 7 cows, at one time, from the pasture to the barn. On Tuesday, Bill herded 3 times as many cows from the meadow to the lake. How many cows did Bill herd on Tuesday?

3. The Western Railroad Company asked Pecos Bill to build some railway stations for them. In August, Bill built 6 stations. In September, he built 4 times as many stations (he had a little help from his friends). How many railway stations did Bill (and his friends) build in September?

B. *On a separate piece of paper, write a story problem for your friends to solve by using multiplication. You can make the problem about someone who does amazing things.*

(Supports Student Book D, page 47) **Solving problems logically; understanding mathematical concepts (multiplication).** Students can work independently or in pairs. Provide manipulatives (counters) to aid them. If necessary, define *lasso.* Exercise B can be pair- or small-group work.

A. *Take a survey. Find out what your friends love or hate for lunch. Then fill in the chart.*

| Name | IN MY LUNCH | |
	I Love	I Hate

B. *Describe your favorite breakfast, lunch, and dinner. Use complete sentences.*

Breakfast

_____

_____

Lunch

_____

_____

Dinner

_____

_____

© Addison-Wesley Publishing Company

(Supports Student Book D, page 48) **Home-School Connection; data collection; conducting a survey; using a chart to record information; socializing; comparing /contrasting.** After students fill in charts, they can report to the class. You may want to suggest a sentence pattern for Exercise B; e.g., "For breakfast, I love to eat. . . ." Have students take this page home to share with their families.

Poetry Fun

Write a poem. Choose words from the list below to complete the lines. Read the choices aloud to see which words sound the best to you. You can choose words of your own, too. Give your poem a title. Copy it on a separate piece of paper and illustrate it.

_____

(Title)

Mary _____ had crackers and tea;
       1

The crackers were _____,
                  2

So she ate _____.
           3

Then for dessert, the _____ looked nice.
                      4

She mixed them with _____,
                    5

And _____, and _____.
     6   7

"A wonderful _____," Mary then said,
             8

And rose from the _____
                  9

And stood on her _____!
                 10

1. Scary	2. tiny	3. ninety-three	4. carrots
Hairy	huge	thirty-three	turnips
5. ketchup	6. pickles	7. rice	8. meal
lettuce	apples	ice	snack
9. table	10. head		
chair	bed		

(Supports Student Book D, page 49) **Creating rhymes; experiencing rhythm and cadence.** After students make their poetic choices, volunteers can read their poems aloud. Compare differences in word choices. Some students may want to try writing original poems about food. You may want to save this page in the student's **Assessment Portfolio.**

43

A Answer the questions about the story on student page 50.

1. Who came to the mattress factory? _____

2. Was the boss a man or a woman? _____

3. What did the boss tell the secretary to do? _____

4. What did the boss find the next day? _____

5. Was the secretary a man or a woman? _____

6. Was the worker happy or sad? _____

7. Who had an idea? _____

8. Why was the boss angry? _____

9. What did the secretary write? _____

Fill in the blanks with **have, has,** *or* **had.**

1. I'm sorry. I _____ to go now.

2. Peter _____ to go home early yesterday.

3. Susanna _____ to help her mother tomorrow.

4. I _____ to walk to school when I was young.

5. Mother _____ to stop at the bank before she goes to town.

6. Father _____ to buy gas before he drove to work.

7. We _____ to hurry or we'll be late.

(Supports Student Book D, pages 50-51) **Reading for a purpose; expressing obligation.** Students work individually and then correct orally in class.

Answer the questions. Use complete sentences.

1. When do you have to go? (now)   *I have to go now.*

2. When does she have to study?
   (every day) _____

3. When do they have to go to bed?
   (at nine) _____

4. When did you have to cook dinner?
   (yesterday) _____

5. When do they have to eat lunch?
   (at one) _____

6. When did you have to see him?
   (last week) _____

Fill in the blanks with **can't** *or* **couldn't.**

1. I _____ swim now, but I want to learn how.

2. I _____ walk when I was six months old.

3. They _____ help me yesterday.

4. We _____ do everything you ask us to do.

5. You _____ come yesterday. Why not?

6. He _____ come tomorrow, I'm sorry to say.

7. We _____ go to Spain last year, but we're going this year.

8. He _____ stop what he's doing now.

Write three things you **have** *to do every day.*	*Write three things you* **can't** *do now (but maybe you'll learn how).*	*Write three things you* **couldn't** *do when you were a baby.*
_____	_____	_____
_____	_____	_____
_____	_____	_____

(Supports Student Book D, pages 50-51) **Expressing obligation; expressing inability, present and past; relating personal experience.** Instruct students to use phrases in parentheses to answer the questions in the first exercise. The second exercise can be used for dialogue practice. Brainstorm ideas for the third exercise, and share answers in class.

A. *Write a short article about a sports star who you think is amazing. Tell why he or she is a favorite of yours. Cut out a photo of the athlete from a magazine and paste it in the box. Or draw your star in action.*

_____

_____

_____

_____

_____

_____

_____

_____

(Supports Student Book D, page 52) **Report writing; organizational planning; expressing ideas through art.** Discuss briefly how an article (nonfiction) is different from a story (fiction). You may want to have students share their articles and artwork. Post on class bulletin board. You may want to save this page in the student's **Assessment Portfolio.**

B. *Think of an amazing, crazy invention, and draw a picture of it.*
Explain each step in your invention. If it has parts, label them
with numbers or letters. Use one of these suggestions, or come
up with your own idea.

a toothbrush for pets
a banana peeler
a three-wheeled automobile
a window-washing machine

(Supports Student Book D, page 53) **Creative art activity; organizational planning; imagery.** Have students brainstorm in small groups to get ideas for their "inventions." They can work individually, in pairs, or in groups. Post artwork on class bulletin board. You may want to save this page in the student's **Assessment Portfolio**.

47

A Fill in the blanks to finish the conversations. Then practice the conversations with a partner.

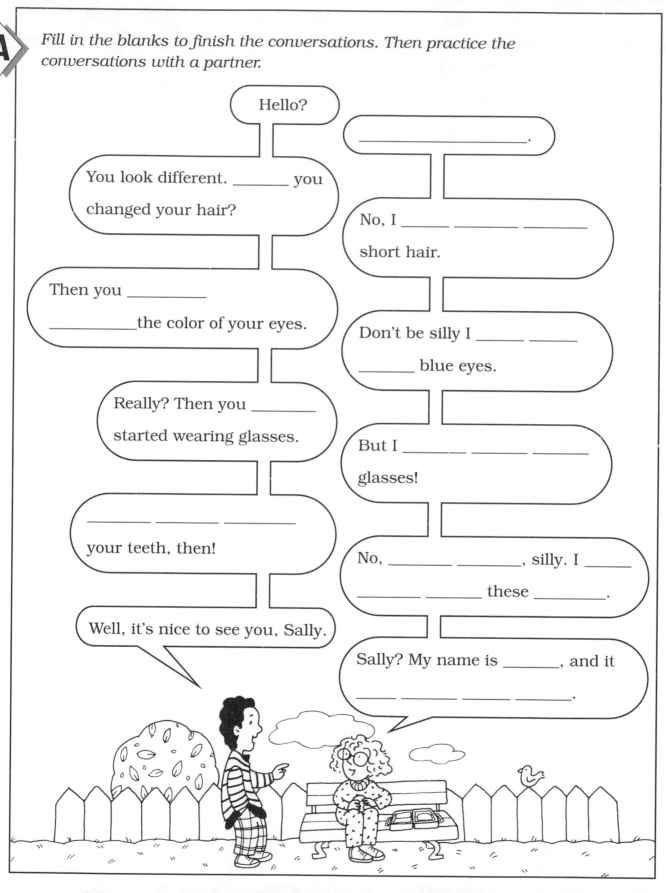

Hello?

_____.

You look different. _____ you changed your hair?

No, I _____ _____ _____ short hair.

Then you _____ _____ the color of your eyes.

Don't be silly I _____ _____ _____ blue eyes.

Really? Then you _____ started wearing glasses.

But I _____ _____ _____ glasses!

_____ _____ _____ your teeth, then!

No, _____ _____, silly. I _____ _____ _____ these _____.

Well, it's nice to see you, Sally.

Sally? My name is _____, and it _____ _____ _____ _____.

(Supports Student Book D, page 54) **Present perfect tense; role-playing fixed and free dialogues; creating new dialogues from cues; socializing.** Have students work in pairs to complete the dialogues. They may need to refer to their student books. Partners can practice completed dialogues.

B Look at the model conversations. Then make new conversations, using the information below. Work with a partner.

★ Tom has changed.
● What do you mean?
★ Well, he's tall now.
● But Tom has always been tall!

★ The twins have changed.
● What do you mean?
★ They wear glasses now.
● But they have always worn glasses.

1. _____
_____

Well, Max is funny now.

2. _____
_____

Betty and Ben are cute now.

3. _____
_____

Well, you're tall now.

4. _____
_____

Sara is thin now.

5. _____
_____

Well, Kim wears earrings now.

6. _____
_____

You are smart now.

© Addison-Wesley Publishing Company

(Supports Student Book D, page 55) **Present perfect tense; creating new dialogues from cues.** Have students work in pairs. Check answers in class. Then students can practice corrected dialogues.

Choose one huge dinosaur and one small one. Write the name of each dinosaur and three amazing facts about it. Draw pictures of your dinosaurs.

Huge Dinosaur   **Small Dinosaur**

_____   _____

1. _____   1. _____

2. _____   2. _____

3. _____   3. _____

(Supports Student Book D, page 56) **Research; note-taking; report writing; learning through art.** Refer students to appropriate resources. You may want to make this pairwork or a small-group project. Post students' facts and artwork on class bulletin board. You may want to save this page in the student's **Assessment Portfolio**.

*What other animals were alive when dinosaurs ruled the earth?
Were these animals enemies of the dinosaurs? Were they the
dinosaurs' food? What did these animals eat? Are they now extinct,
too? Find out whatever you can, and write the information here.*

_____

_____

_____

_____

_____

_____

_____

_____

_____

_____

_____

_____

_____

_____

_____

_____

_____

(Supports Student Book D, page 57) **Research; note-taking; report writing.** Refer students to appropriate
resources. You may want to make this pairwork or a small-group project. You may want to save this page in
the student's **Assessment Portfolio**.

Hot, Hot, Really Hot, Red Hot Peppers

Use your student book to find answers to the questions about the story. Write your answers on a separate piece of paper.

1. What was the old woman doing before the huge, hungry tiger came out of the forest?

2. Did the old woman tell the tiger she was too fat to make him a good meal?

3. What did the old woman cook in her pot?

4. What rolled down the old woman's cheeks while she was eating?

5. Which came first to the old woman's door, the enormous white egg or the large yellow banana?

6. Which came last to the old woman's door, the big brown mat or the fat red rope?

7. What time did the old woman say the tiger was coming to eat her up?

8. What did the tiger take a giant mouthful of?

9. What happened when the tiger landed on the banana peel?

10. What did the egg do?

11. What did the mat do?

12. What did the rope do?

13. How many soldiers came to take the tiger away?

14. Why did the old woman cry while she ate her huge lunch?

(Supports Student Book D, pages 58-63) **Understanding details in a story; understanding cause and effect; understanding sequence; making inferences.** Accept long or short answers. After students complete exercise independently, correct in class. Discuss spicy-food likes and dislikes.

Hot, Hot, Really Hot, Red Hot Peppers

"Hot, Hot, Really Hot, Red Hot Peppers" is a fantasy—it didn't really happen. Write your own amazing fantasy. Imagine that you are in danger. Who or what is coming to get you? Who or what will help you? How? Give your story a title. Then illustrate your story.

_____

(Title)

_____

_____

_____

_____

_____

_____

_____

_____

_____

(Supports Student Book D, pages 58-63) **Creative writing; discussing fears/fantasies; using past tense; expressing ideas through art.** If necessary, help students use past tense. They can exchange papers for peer comment/correction and then share with class.

Alice and Humpty Dumpty

*Use the words in the Data Bank. Finish the paragraphs about
Alice and Humpty Dumpty.*

Humpty Dumpty was sitting on the top of a _____ wall. Alice

_____ how he could keep his _____.

"How exactly like an egg he is," Alice said _____.

"It's very **provoking**," Humpty Dumpty _____ after a long silence, "to

be called an _____."

"I said you **looked** like an egg, Sir. Some eggs are _____ pretty, you

know. And _____ a beautiful belt _____ got on! At least, a beautiful

tie, I should have said—no, a belt, I mean . . ."

She stopped. Humpty Dumpty _____ very angry. He said _____

for a minute or two.

"It is a—**most—provoking—thing**," he said at last, "when a person

_____ know a necktie from a belt!"

"I know it's very ignorant of me," _____ said.

(If only _____ knew, she thought, which is his

neck and _____ is his waist!)

DATA BANK

balance	very	nothing
doesn't	which	I
Alice	looked	aloud
high	wondered	egg
said	what	you've

(Supports Student Book D, page 64) **Reading comprehension; cloze exercise; syntax.** Students read sentences from the story they listened to on student book page 64. This exercise provides an opportunity for students to review the story and to learn syntax. Correct in class. You may want to save this page in the student's **Assessment Portfolio.**

Make an Amazing Facts game of your own. Use facts from this book and your student book. You can write new facts, too. Write your questions in the squares. Write the correct answers on a separate piece of paper. Ask your teacher to check your game before you exchange games and play with friends.

(Supports Student Book D, page 66) **Creating a game; research; note-taking; socializing.** Encourage students to research answers they don't know. Store games in a box students can access during free time.

A. Write your ideas and thoughts about the unit theme, "Stories Across Time." What do you think the unit will be about? Do you like to learn about things that happened in the past? Are you curious about people and places around the world?

_____

_____

_____

_____

_____

_____

_____

_____

_____

B. As you go through the unit, write your thoughts about each page. What would you like to find out more about? Use extra paper if you need more space.

_____

_____

_____

_____

_____

_____

_____

_____

(Supports Student Book D, page 67) **Prewriting; predicting**. In Exercise A, students write their thoughts after participating in the class discussion of the unit opener page. Encourage students to come back to this page periodically to complete Exercise B. You may want to save this page in the student's **Assessment Portfolio**.

C. Use the notes and ideas you wrote on page 56 to write about "Stories Across Time." What did you like most in the unit? Why? What did you like least? Why? What did you learn?

_____

_____

_____

_____

_____

_____

_____

_____

_____

_____

_____

_____

_____

_____

_____

_____

_____

_____

_____

_____

© Addison-Wesley Publishing Company

(Supports Student Book D, Theme 4. Use after page 86.) **Writing opinions; using notes; recalling details; summarizing; self-assessment.** This page provides an opportunity for students to sum up their thoughts about the unit and to tell what they learned. You may want to save this page in the student's **Assessment Portfolio**.

● ● ● ● ●

A. *Write the words for the numbers. Check your student book if you need help.*

1. lst   _____

2. 2nd   _____

3. 3rd   _____

4. 4th   _____

5. 5th   _____

6. 6th   _____

7. 7th   _____

8. 8th   _____

9. 9th   _____

10. 10th   _____

11. 11th   _____

12. 12th   _____

13. 13th   _____

14. 14th   _____

15. 20th   _____

16. 21st   _____

17. 22nd   _____

18. 30th   _____

19. 40th   _____

20. 50th   _____

B. *Fill in the blanks with **before, after,** or one of the words from Exercise A.*

1. February comes _____ March. It's the _____ month of the year.

2. August comes _____ July. It's the _____ month of the year.

3. December comes _____ November. It's the _____ month of the year.

4. June comes _____ May. It's the _____ month of the year.

5. October comes _____ September. It's the _____ month of the year.

(Supports Student Book D, page 68) **Ordinal numbers; sequencing.** For Exercise A, warn students that the ordinal numbers do not match the exercise item numbers after 14. After students complete Exercise A independently, have them work in pairs to complete Exercise B.

PROBLEM SOLVING

A. **Archaeology** is the study of past human life. Archaeologists study **artifacts,** objects that were made or used by people in the past. A pottery bowl is an example of an artifact. The place where archaeologists dig for artifacts is called a **site.**

The circle graph shows how a whole is divided into parts. Look at the artifacts graph and answer the questions.

1. Which artifact was found the most often?

   _____

2. Which artifact was found the least often?

   _____

3. Does pottery total half, more than half, or less than half of the artifacts found at the site?

   _____

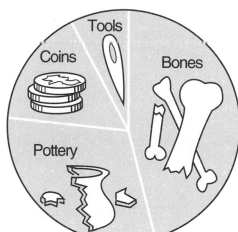

B. *Work with a partner. Look at the circle graph showing Susan's typical school day. Then write questions about Susan's day on the lines. Answer each other's questions.*

_____

_____

_____

_____

_____

_____

_____

_____

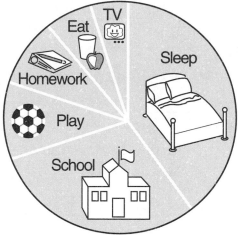

(Supports Student Book D, page 69) **Solving problems logically; interpreting graphs; conceptualizing greater than/less than; asking/answering questions.** Go over Exercise A with the class before assigning Exercise B. As an extension, have students make graphs reflecting their typical school day.

A. *Read about what's good to grow—and eat—in Mexico. Then answer the questions.*

Before European settlers came to Mexico, the Indians there had learned to grow a wide variety of crops. These included maize (corn), squash, sweet potatoes, avocados, peppers, beans, vanilla, chiles, chocolate, and tomatoes.

Today, farmers in Mexico grow wheat, coffee, bananas, beans, cotton, oranges, potatoes, and sugar cane. Mexican forests supply timber for pulp and paper. And the Sapodilla tree provides **chicle**—used to make chewing gum.

But the favorite crop of the Mexican farmer is corn. In fact, more land is used to grow corn than any other crop in Mexico. **Tortillas,** the bread of Mexico, are made of cornmeal. You can put almost any kind of food into a tortilla, fold it or roll it up, and have a wonderful meal. Tortillas are delicious just plain, too.

1. *Circle **True** or **False:*** The most popular crop among farmers in Mexico today is bananas.

2. Name three crops other than corn that the Indians of Mexico knew how to grow before Europeans arrived.

_____

3. What is typical Mexican bread called?

_____

4. What can you do with it?

_____

5. Name three crops other than corn that farmers grow in Mexico today.

_____

B. *Find out more about Mexico. Write the information on a separate piece of paper. Be sure to answer these questions: What is the capital of the country? How many people live in Mexico? What other countries does Mexico share a border with? What continent does Mexico belong to?*

(Supports Student Book D, page 70) **Reading for a purpose; research; note-taking.** Correct Exercise A in class. Accept long or short answers. You may want to assign Exercise B as small-group work.

Poetry Fun

A. Look at the poem "The Meal," on page 49 of your student book. It has words that rhyme with each other. Some poems do not have rhyming words. The poem about the Toltec Indians on page 71 of your student book does **not** rhyme. It is an example of **free verse**.

Here is another example of free verse. It's a Navajo poem, to be sung or chanted.

After you have read the poem two or three times, answer the questions.

My great corn plants,
Among them I walk.
I speak to them,
They hold out their hands to me.

Navajo

1. What is the poet speaking to? Why?

_____

2. Whose hands is the poet talking about? Do they really have hands?

_____

3. What is surprising about the poem?

_____

B. *Try writing a free-verse poem. Use a separate piece of paper. You might write about a pet, your favorite season, a family member or a friend—or anything else that's important to you.*

(Supports Student Book D, page 71) **Creating verse; learning language through poems and songs; enjoying figurative language.** You might want to discuss *personification* with students. Before assigning Exercise B, brainstorm ideas with whole class. Have students share their poems as appropriate.

61

A Compare these two scenes. Find as many differences as you can.

Scene 1

Scene 2

_____   _____

_____   _____

_____   _____

_____   _____

_____   _____

_____   _____

_____   _____

_____   _____

_____   _____

_____   _____

_____   _____

(Supports Student Book D, page 72) **Identifying plural nouns.** Students work in pairs to find singular/plural differences. One student can be the "secretary" and write down the singular and plural forms. Which pair of students can find the most differences in a "speed drill" of five to ten minutes? Help students with unfamiliar vocabulary.

Complete the sentences about the story on student page 73.

1. Ali Baba was so poor that he had no rice and no _____.

2. His wife asked him to look for _____.

3. Ali slept in a tree because he was afraid of _____.

4. When Ali woke up he saw forty _____.

5. In the cave Ali saw _____ all around the walls.

6. The forty thieves arrived with their _____ between their _____.

Fill in the blanks, using the plural forms of the words in the Data Bank.

DATA BANK

knife	woman	tooth	shelf	wife	man	leaf

1. Humans and gorillas have the same number of _____.

2. When we set the table, we put forks to the left of the plate and _____ and spoons to the right.

3. In the fall, the _____ change color and fall off the trees.

4. How many _____ does your new bookcase have?

5. When people get married, the _____ become the husbands, and the _____ become the _____.

Make up a short story, using as many of the plural words in the Data Bank as you can. Can you make the story funny? Make notes and write your story on a separate piece of paper.

DATA BANK

babies	candies	women	mice
children	feet	halves	monkeys

(Supports Student Book D, page 73) **Plural nouns; creative writing.** Students work in pairs or individually to complete exercises. They might enjoy writing a story as a "team."

A. *Match the words with their definitions. Write the correct letter on the line. You may need to use a dictionary.*

1. spear _____   a. top layer

2. region _____   b. to save from danger

3. border _____   c. to leak out slowly

4. rescue _____   d. long tool or weapon with a sharp point

5. surface _____   e. particular area or place

6. prehistoric _____   f. to melt away

7. seep _____   g. before recorded history or writing

8. dissolve _____   h. area separating two geographic places

B. *Can you find more amazing facts about the Stone Age? Number them and write them here. Be prepared to share your information with the class.*

_____

_____

_____

_____

_____

_____

_____

_____

_____

_____

_____

_____

(Supports Student Book D, pages 74-75) **Vocabulary development; using a dictionary; research; note-taking; making oral reports.** After students complete Exercise A, have them exchange papers to correct. Students can present facts about the Stone Age orally. You may want to save this page in the student's **Assessment Portfolio**.

C. How would you like to be in a cave with several **million** bats? If you visit Carlsbad Caverns during the summer, the residents of Bat Cave will be there to greet you.

Read more amazing information about Carlsbad Caverns, and then answer the questions.

Carlsbad Caverns are located in a national park in the state of New Mexico. The caverns, or caves, extend for miles and miles under the park. No one knows how far they go, but about 21 miles (33.5 kilometers) of the main cavern have been explored so far. This cavern is divided into three major levels. The first, or deepest, level is 1,027 feet (313 meters) underground. Visitors can go down 750 feet (230 meters). How do they descend? By elevator!

The caves were formed when water dissolved the underground layers of rock called **limestone**. When the water evaporated, mineral deposits were left. Icicle-shaped mineral deposits hang from the ceilings of the caves. These are called **stalactites**. Sprouting up from the cave floors are similar mineral deposits, called **stalagmites**. Try to remember which is which!

1. What state are the Carlsbad Caverns located in?

_____

2. *Circle **True** or **False:*** The Carlsbad Caverns have been completely explored.

3. *Circle **True** or **False:*** Stalactites and stalagmites are both made of mineral deposits.

4. What kind of rock dissolved to form the mineral deposits in the caves?

_____

5. How far down in the main cavern can visitors go? How do they get there?

_____

(Supports Student Book D, pages 74-75) **Reading for a purpose; vocabulary development.** Accept long or short answers. Correct in class. As an extension, have students research spelunking. You may want to save this page in the student's **Assessment Portfolio**.

A Ask your partner these questions.
Write down his or her answers.

1. How do you feel today?   My partner *feels great*   .

2. What time did you leave for   My partner _____.
   school this morning?

3. What do you keep in your   My partner _____.
   notebook?

4. How did you feel yesterday?   My partner _____.

5. When do you sleep late?   My partner _____.

Look at the pictures and answer the questions.
Use complete sentences.

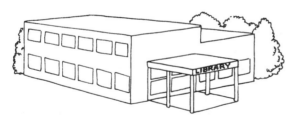

1. What did Lisa send her son?

   _____

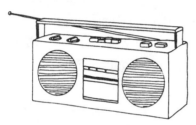

2. What did the architect build?

   _____

3. Where did Jan sleep?

   _____

4. Where did the boat sink?

   _____

66

(Supports Student Book D, page 76) **Irregular verb forms.** For the first exercise, students work in pairs and interview each other. They work independently to write complete-sentence answers for the second exercise. (Encourage them to use pronouns.) For question 4, accept *water* if students do not know the word *bathtub.*

Answer the questions about the story on student page 77. Use complete sentences.

1. Where was the island that Don, Wayne, and Warren were shipwrecked on?   _____

2. What did they build?   _____

3. Where did they sleep?   _____

4, What did they think?   _____

_____

Write **True** *or* **False** *after each sentence.*

1. They wrote messages in the sand.   _____

2. They sent messages in bottles.   _____

3. They felt better and better.   _____

4. They thought about going on vacation.   _____

5. Don found a bottle on the beach.   _____

_____

Find the mistakes and write the sentences correctly.

1. Warren jumped out of the bottle.

_____

2. The genie was captive in the bottle for 100 years.

_____

3. The genie gave the men ten wishes each.

_____

4. Warren wanted to stay on the island.

_____

5. Wayne was lonely without Don and Warren.

_____

(Supports Student Book D, page 77) **Reading for a purpose; irregular verb forms; distinguishing true-false statements.** Students work independently to complete exercises. They can exchange papers with other students for correction; or correct as whole class.

A. *Match the capital cities with the states. Write the correct letter on the line. Use a map or an atlas if you're not sure of an answer.*

1. Sacramento _____   a. Alaska

2. Tallahassee _____   b. New York

3. Juneau _____   c. Hawaii

4. Albany _____   d. Tennessee

5. Nashville _____   e. Arizona

6. Honolulu _____   f. California

7. Olympia _____   g. Florida

8. Phoenix _____   h. Washington

B. *Now try the whole world! Match capital cities with their countries. Write the correct letter on the line.*

1. Ottawa _____   a. Venezuela

2. Seoul _____   b. Italy

3. Madrid _____   c. Spain

4. Mexico City _____   d. Japan

5. Tokyo _____   e. South Korea

6. Rome _____   f. Taiwan

7. Taipei _____   g. Canada

8. Caracas _____   h. Mexico

(Supports Student Book D, page 78) **Exploring U.S. and world geography; research.** Refer students to appropriate references. Students can work independently or in pairs to complete the exercises. Correct in class.

Choose one of the countries on page 68. Or choose another country. Plan a trip there! Who will go with you on your trip? What cities besides the capital will you visit? What famous buildings or other places will you see? What kind of food will you eat? What will the weather be like?

Answer the questions above and write all about your amazing trip. Use extra paper if you need more space.

_____

_____

_____

_____

_____

_____

_____

_____

_____

_____

_____

_____

_____

(Supports Student Book D, page 79) **Home-School Connection; research; note-taking; report writing; exploring world geography; appreciating multicultural diversity.** Help students find appropriate reference materials. You may want to have students give oral reports on their "trips." You may want to save a copy of this page in the student's **Assessment Portfolio**. Have students take this page home to share with their families.

The Land I Lost

Circle the letter of the correct answer.

1. Where was the village?
   a. By a lake
   b. By a river
   c. On a mountain
   d. In the jungle

2. How many houses were in the village?
   a. Fifteen   c. Fifty
   b. Five hundred   d. Five

3. How did you get into the house?
   a. You walked up some stairs
   b. You walked across a bridge.
   c. You jumped over a trench.
   d. You jumped from a bamboo tree.

4. What did the people do at night?
   a. They locked the door.
   b. They put up bars.
   c. They pulled in a stick.
   d. They pulled in the bridge.

5. Where was the nearest shop?
   a. In the village
   b. Over the mountains
   c. Across the river
   d. In the city

6. What did they do in the dry season?
   a. They planted rice and potatoes.
   b. They played or slept at home.
   c. They went to school every day.
   d. They hunted in the jungle.

7. How long was the rainy season?
   a. Most of the year
   b. Three or four months
   c. About half the year
   d. Very short—just a month

8. When did children first begin to work?
   a. As soon as they could walk
   b. At the age of three or four
   c. When they were six years old
   d. Before they started school

9. How did the children learn to read?
   a. They had a private teacher.
   b. Mother taught them.
   c. Father gave them lessons.
   d. They studied together.

10. What did Huynh Quang Nhuong want to become?
    a. A farmer   c. A hunter
    b. A doctor   d. A teacher

(Supports Student Book D, pages 80-83) **Multiple-choice questions**. Check answers in class.

The Land I Lost

Answer the questions. Use complete sentences.

1. What is your full name?

_____

2. Where were you born?

_____

3. Where were your parents born?

_____

4. What is your native language?

_____

5. Do you enjoy speaking English?

_____

6. When did your family come to this country?

_____

_____

7. Do you have a lot of relatives in this country? Who are they? (grandparents? uncles? aunts? cousins?)

_____

_____

_____

8. Have you ever returned to your native country for a visit?

_____

_____

_____

(Supports Student Book D, pages 80-83) **Home-School Connection; writing/talking about personal experiences.** Students can use the exercise to interview each other. Decide in advance which questions may be inappropriate for your class—because they are irrelevant or possibly too intrusive. You may want to save a copy of this page in the student's **Assessment Portfolio**. Have students take this page home to share with their families.

71

Pioneer School

Use the words in the Data Bank. Finish the paragraphs about the pioneer school.

Roxana Rice and her brother Earl sat on a _____ wooden

bench. Near _____ was a cast-iron stove that kept the whole

room warm. They were at school. It was a one-room schoolhouse

in _____.

Roxana looked _____. Many other boys and girls of all

ages _____ on other benches. The _____ were noisy.

Some whistled and _____ things at each other. Roxana's

family dog, Boxy, was standing at the _____. He was

whining _____ he wanted to come in and sleep by Roxana's

_____. Just as Roxana got up to pet Boxy, Earl pulled her

back down.

"No, Roxana," he said. "Look, our _____ here."

_____ Morrison, the teacher, walked into the room. He

was _____ sixteen years old. Many _____ in frontier

schools were teenagers. Soon Mr. Morrison _____ the

arithmetic lesson.

DATA BANK

Mr.	only	teachers
door	threw	children
began	hard	feet
teacher's	Kansas	sat
them	around	because

(Supports Student Book D, page 84) **Reading comprehension; cloze exercise; syntax.** Students read sentences from the story they listened to on student book page 84. This exercise provides an opportunity for students to review the story and to learn syntax. Correct in class. You may want to save this page in the student's **Assessment Portfolio**.

Make an Amazing Facts game of your own. Use facts from this book and your student book. You can write new facts, too. Write your questions in the squares. Write the correct answers on a separate piece of paper. Ask your teacher to check your game before you exchange games and play with friends.

(Supports Student Book D, page 86) **Creating a game; research; note-taking; socializing.** Encourage students to research answers they don't know. Store games in a box students can access during free time.

73

A. Write your ideas and thoughts about the unit theme, "Animals Around Us." What do you think the unit will be about? What are your favorite animals? Do you have a pet at home? Do you like to read stories about animals? Which are your favorites?

_____

_____

_____

_____

_____

_____

_____

_____

_____

B. As you go through the unit, write your thoughts about each page. What would you like to find out more about? Use extra paper if you need more space.

_____

_____

_____

_____

_____

_____

_____

_____

(Supports Student Book D, page 87) **Prewriting; predicting.** In Exercise A, students write their thoughts after participating in the class discussion of the unit opener page. Encourage students to come back to this page periodically to complete Exercise B. You may want to save this page in the student's **Assessment Portfolio**.

C. Use the notes and ideas you wrote on page 74 to write about "Animals Around Us." What did you like most in the unit? Why? What did you like least? Why? What did you learn?

(Supports Student Book D, Theme 5. Use after page 106.) **Writing opinions; using notes; recalling details; summarizing; self-assessment.** This page provides an opportunity for students to sum up their thoughts about the unit and to tell what they learned. You may want to save this page in the student's **Assessment Portfolio**.

A. *Circle the letter of the best response.*

1. Can I help you?
   a. I'd like tickets for the show.
   b. Just a few, please.
   c. Here you are.

2. For which day?
   a. In the afternoon.
   b. Tomorrow.
   c. The evening show.

3. For which show?
   a. The evening game.
   b. The important game.
   c. The evening one.

4. How many seats?
   a. Two adults and one child, please.
   b. Two chairs and one table, please.
   c. Here's your change.

B. *Read carefully and complete the conversation.*

Have you still got tickets for the show?   *Yes, a few.* _____

For Monday?   _____?

The afternoon show.   _____?

Three tickets, please.   _____?

Two children, one adult.   _____.

C. *Look at the poster and answer the questions.*

Sharing a Song

Shows Wednesday

10:00 a.m.   2:00 p.m.   8:00 p.m.

Adults: $5.75
Children under 12: $3.00

1. What day can you go?

_____

2. How many shows are there?

_____

3. How much does it cost for your mother?

_____

4. How much does it cost for your eight-year-old sister?

_____

((Supports Student Book D, page 88) **Understanding sequence in conversations; finding out information.**
Exercises A and B can be used for dialogue practice after students complete independently.

PROBLEM SOLVING

A. *Rosa lives on a farm. Her family has 9 cows. Look at the polygons Rosa used to fence in the cows. Add 1 polygon to the corral to help her keep each cow in its own pen. (Hint: Draw your polygon on tracing paper to use over the corral.)*

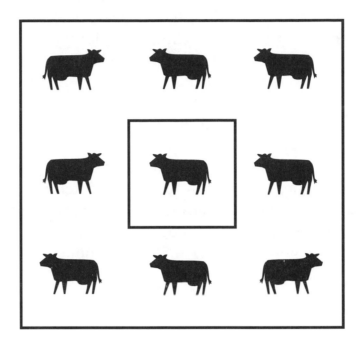

B. *Rosa's family also has sheep on the farm. Help Rosa divide this corral into 4 equal pens for the sheep. Draw 4 fences Rosa can build to create 4 smaller polygons that look exactly like the corral. Your polygons should fit inside the corral without overlapping each other.*

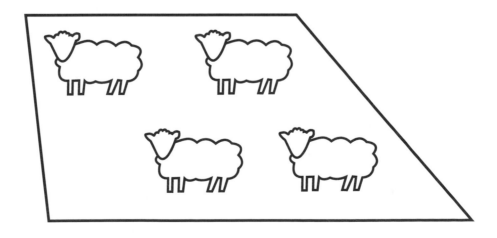

(Supports Student Book D, page 89) **Solving problems logically; learning mathematical concepts (geometry).** Explain that a polygon is a plane, or flat, figure whose sides are straight and connected. You may want to have students work in pairs to solve the problems. Correct in class.

77

A. *Believe it or not! Read about these amazing animals, and then answer the questions.*

Have you ever heard of a duck-billed platypus? The platypus is an animal that lives only in Australia. Its body is something like a large mole's, but its beak is like a duck's beak. And, like a duck, it has webbed feet for swimming. The platypus is unusual because its babies are hatched from an egg, like birds, but the babies are nursed on their mother's milk, like mammals. What does the platypus eat? As it swims underwater, it finds small crabs, worms, and mollusks with its beak.

What's round, about 1 foot long, half an inch wide, and sticky? Give up? The answer is the tongue of the great anteater. With its sticky tongue, the great anteater can catch and eat hundreds of insects at once. After dinner, the anteater rolls itself into a ball and, using its tail as a blanket, goes to sleep for the rest of the day. The great anteater makes its home along the Amazon River, in South America.

1. In what two ways does the platypus look like a duck?

_____

2. *Circle* **True** *or* **False:** Platypus babies are hatched from eggs.

3. *Circle* **True** *or* **False:** Platypus babies are nursed on their mother's milk.

4. What body part does the platypus use to find its food?

_____

5. What does the anteater use to catch and eat insects?

_____

6. What does the anteater do when it finishes its dinner?

_____

B. *Find out more about animals that live on the Amazon River. Choose one of these animals (or another one):* **the jaguar, the ocelot, the puma, the caiman.** *Write your information on a separate piece of paper.*

(Supports Student Book D, page 90) **Reading for a purpose; research; note-taking.** Correct Exercise A in class. Accept long or short answers. Students can make oral reports based on their research for Exercise B. You may want to save this page in the student's **Assessment Portfolio.**

The Dog and the Bone

A. *Answer the questions about the story on student page 91.*

1. What was the dog carrying? _____

2. What did he do on the bridge? _____

3. What did he see in the water? _____

4. What did he think he saw? _____

5. What did he think the other dog had? _____

6. What did he do to frighten the
   other dog? _____

7. What happened when he opened
   his mouth? _____

B. *What's wrong with this picture? Find five things that
are wrong.*

1. _____

2. _____

3. _____

4. _____

5. _____

(Supports Student Book D, page 91) **Past tense forms.** Students use fable to answer the questions in
Exercise A. Encourage them to use complete sentences. "Began to bark" or "barked" are both acceptable for
number 6. Students can "solve" Exercise B, which they are to compare with fable, in pairs or individually.

79

A *Look at the pictures and answer the questions.*

1. What did the elephant try to do?

_____

_____

2. What did the girls play?

_____

_____

3. Where did the bus stop?

_____

_____

4. Where did he jog?

_____

_____

5. What did he carry?

_____

_____

(Supports Student Book D, page 92) **Simple past tense regular forms; matching pictures and written text; comprehension questions.** Students work independently, then correct in class.

Answer the questions, as in the example.

Example: Didn't Frank play baseball today? (basketball)
No, he didn't. He played basketball.

1. Didn't Paula jog in the park today? (gym)

_____

2. Didn't the Changs carry their tents from the campground? (backpacks)

_____

3. Didn't Ms. Lopez employ 200 people last year? (50 people)

_____

Answer the questions about the story on page 93 of your student book. Use complete sentences.

1. What did Max pack?

_____

2. What room did Max check first?

_____

3. What did Charlie turn off?

_____

4. What did Charlie unplug?

_____

5. What did Charlie do to the bathtub?

_____

6. What did Charlie do with the toys?

_____

(Supports Student Book D, page 93) **Simple past tense.** Have students work independently, then correct in class. Encourage them to use pronouns. Students may want to make up more examples for the first exercise; have them use the verbs on student page 92.

A. *Review pages 94-95 of your student book to answer the questions about animals.*

1. Where does the electric eel live?

_____

2. Where is the eel's brain?

_____

3. What can knock a grown man down?

_____

4. *Fill in the blanks:* During the life cycle of a butterfly, it is first an

_____. Next, it becomes a _____. Then it becomes a _____.

Finally, it turns into a _____.

5. When does a butterfly eat the most?

_____

6. *Circle* **True** *or* **False:** A rhinoceros has better eyesight than a hippo.

7. What does a hippo do when it sees trouble coming?

_____

8. How do bees talk to one another?

_____

B. *Find out more about* **metamorphosis.** *On a separate piece of paper, write an article about what you learned. Share the information with your family and friends.*

(Supports Student Book D, pages 94-95) **Reading for a purpose; sequencing (question 4); research; note-taking; report writing.** Accept short answers. Correct and discuss in class. Students can work in pairs or small groups to write their reports. You may want to save this page in the student's **Assessment Portfolio.**

C. *How many animal names can you find? First, write in the letters to complete the animal names. Then find the names and circle them in the puzzle.*

ALL____GATOR   ____ABBIT   GOR____LL____

B____AR   R____ ____STER   H____PP____P____T____M____S

CA____EL   S____AL   HO____SE

____EER   SH____RK   KANGAR____ ____

D____G   SN____K____   LI____N

D____NK____Y   TIG____R   M____NK____Y

E____GL____   T____RTLE   M____USE

ELEP____ANT   WH____LE   P____NDA

FO____   ZEB____A   P____L____R B____AR

GI____AFF____

Animals I Know

K	D	X	H	I	P	P	O	P	O	T	A	M	U	S
A	O	M	O	N	K	E	Y	O	N	F	O	X	T	N
N	G	B	T	C	A	M	E	L	F	Z	E	B	R	A
G	D	E	E	R	D	F	H	A	J	V	R	T	C	K
A	L	L	I	G	A	T	O	R	X	H	O	R	S	E
R	M	E	D	L	I	O	N	B	N	R	S	E	A	L
O	G	P	A	N	D	A	G	E	A	G	L	E	X	G
O	O	H	B	T	H	N	C	A	P	I	B	T	K	D
V	R	A	K	T	I	G	E	R	M	R	C	J	M	O
B	I	N	W	R	J	H	X	S	H	A	R	K	O	N
E	L	T	U	R	T	L	E	T	M	F	P	V	U	K
A	L	M	R	O	O	S	T	E	R	F	K	N	S	E
R	A	B	B	I	T	W	H	A	L	E	P	L	E	Y

(Supports Student Book D, page 95) **Solving a puzzle; vocabulary development.** Students can do word-search puzzle independently or in paris.

83

A *Look at the pictures and answer the questions.*

1. What does she take to work?

_____

_____

2. What did he fall off yesterday?

_____

_____

3. Where does he go every day?

_____

_____

4. When does the game begin?

_____

_____

5. What did the girl break yesterday?

_____

_____

(Supports Student Book D, page 96) **Present and past tense verb forms; matching pictures with written language.** Students work independently. Correct with whole group.

B. *Answer the questions about the story on student page 97. Use a separate piece of paper and answer in complete sentences.*

1. Where did Mike and Bob go?

2. What kind of film was it?

3. What had the outlaws done?

4. What did the sheriff need?

5. Who did the sheriff call?

6. What did the sheriff say?

7. Who was waiting for the marshal?

8. What did the marshal's horse do?

9. Where did the marshal fall?

10. Where did the marshal swim?

11. Who knew what was going to happen?

12. Who didn't think the marshal would fall off his horse again?

Fill in the blanks with the correct form of **see.**

★ Have you _____ this movie before?

● Yes. I've _____ it four times already. It's great!

★ I've _____ it five times.

● Let's stay and _____ it again!

Make up a dialogue like the one above. Use one of these words:
take, throw, know, begin, see.

★ Have you _____ before?

● Yes, I've _____ it _____. _____.

★ I've _____ it _____.

● Let's _____.

© Addison-Wesley Publishing Company

(Supports Student Book D, page 97) **Past tense and past participle; guided dialogues.** While correcting in class, students can "perform" the first exercise as an interview and the second and third exercises as dialogues. They may need help with the third exercise.

Find out more about a special bird. Choose one of these birds: **the eagle, the Canada goose, the barn owl, the hawk.** *Or choose another bird you think is interesting. Write and illustrate an article about your bird.*

(Supports Student Book D, page 98) **Research; note-taking; report writing.** Suggest appropriate reference materials. You may want students to give oral reports on their articles. Post completed work on class bulletin board. You may want to save this page in the student's **Assessment Portfolio.**

THEMEWORK TEAMWORK

Do some research about animals. Then fill in the chart with as many animals as you can. Follow the example. Compare your chart with your friends' charts.

Name of Animal	Wild	Tame	Extinct	Favorite Food	Habitat
walrus	✓			*clams, shrimp, snails, starfish, sea urchins*	*Arctic Ocean*

(Supports Student Book D, page 99) **Data collection; filling in a chart; research; note-taking; comparing/contrasting**. Suggest appropriate reference materials. Tell students to put a check mark where applicable in first three columns. Explain the word *habitat*. Students can compare information. You may want to save this page in the student's **Assessment Portfolio.**

Rabbit and Tiger

It is important for actors to say their lines with feeling. Work with your student book open. Read each part of the play again. Decide how the actor should look or speak or act, and check the best answer.

1. page 100, **Rabbit**: That's true!

   How should Rabbit speak?   ____ in a happy way   ____ in a sad way

2. page 100, **Tiger**: That's not true!

   How should Tiger look?   ____ angry   ____ scared

3. page 101, **Farmer**: Well, that's very kind of you.
   How should the farmer
   speak?   ____ in an angry way   ____ in a friendly way

4. page 101, **Rabbit**: Thank you. That's very nice of you.

   How should Rabbit look?   ____ pleased   ____ angry

5. page 102, **Tiger**: Grr-ah! Now I have you! I'll eat you for lunch!

   How should Tiger look?   ____ surprised   ____ scary

6. page 102, **Tiger**: What? Cheese from the bottom of the lake?

   How should Tiger speak?   ____ in a surprised way   ____ in a sad way

7. page 102, **Rabbit**: Oh, yes. The lake is full of delicious cheese!

   What should Rabbit do?   ____ smile   ____ cry

8. page 103, **Farmer**: Rabbit! Rabbit! I saw the Tiger heading this way.
   How should the farmer
   speak?   ____ in an excited way   ____ in a happy way

9. page 103, **Farmer**: For a delicious piece of cheese? I don't understand.

   How should the farmer look?   ____ puzzled   ____ scared

10. page 103, **Tiger**: Rabbit! Rabbit! Where are you?

    How should Tiger speak?   ____ in an angry way   ____ in a pleased way

(Supports Student Book D, pages 100-103) **Comprehension: using written context to infer character traits.** After students complete the exercise individually, compare answers as a group. Discuss differences of opinion.

Rabbit and Tiger

Write a story about Rabbit and Tiger. Choose words from the choices below and fill in the blanks. You can use other words if you want. Give your story a title.

_____
(title)

One day in _____, Rabbit was _____ under a big _____.
                          1   2   3

Tiger came _____ out of the _____. "Grr-ah!" Tiger
                          4   5

_____. "Rabbit, I'm going to eat you for _____."
      6   7

"Well, first have one of these nice nuts," Rabbit said _____. The
                                                                          8

Tiger tasted the nut. "It's _____," he said. "Tell me where you got
                                        9

these nuts," he _____. "They are growing under the ground in my
                          10

garden," Rabbit said. "I pulled up some weeds, and found the nuts. Please

help yourself," Rabbit said, _____ to himself. "I don't know which
                                          11

weeds are growing nuts and which weeds aren't."

Tiger _____ into the garden and started pulling up weeds.
              12

Rabbit, of course, got up _____ and _____ into the woods.
                                        13   14

1. spring summer	2. sitting lying	3. tree umbrella	4. running jumping	5. woods lake
6. growled roared	7. lunch dinner	8. quickly politely	9. delicious wonderful	10. demanded ordered
11. smiling laughing	12. jumped ran	13. quietly quickly	14. disappeared escaped	

(Supports Student Book D, pages 100-103) **Guided/creative writing; role-playing.** Have students read the vocabulary aloud before assigning this page for independent work. Correct in class after students complete individually. Students can then perform their stories as skits.

A Man, His Son, and a Donkey

Use the words in the Data Bank. Finish the paragraphs about
"A Man, His Son, and a Donkey."

Once there was a man, his wife, and his young son. _____ were

happy, but they _____ more money to buy food and to take _____

of their farm animals. The _____ wife suggested that they sell

_____ donkey.

The man and his son began their walk to town to _____ the donkey

to the market. Soon they met a _____who waved hello and asked, "Are

you crazy? Why are you both walking to town? One of you should be riding

the donkey." So the boy climbed up on the _____ back, and they

continued their walk to town.

Soon they met an old man. The old man _____ hello and asked,

"Why is your son riding the donkey? **You** are the one who should be riding

to town while your son _____." So the boy climbed _____ the

donkey's back, the man climbed _____ the donkey's back, and they

continued their walk to town.

_____ they met an old woman. She waved hello and asked, "Are you

crazy? You should _____ ride on the donkey's back. So the man

_____ on the donkey and helped his son climb up on the

donkey's back.

DATA BANK

on	They	care
waved	man's	off
Soon	donkey's	both
walks	their	friend
stayed	take	needed

(Supports Student Book D, page 104) **Reading comprehension; cloze exercise; syntax.** Students read sentences from the story they listened to on student book page 104. This exercise provides an opportunity for students to review the story and to learn syntax. Correct in class. You may want to save this page in the student's **Assessment Portfolio**.

© Addison-Wesley Publishing Company

Make an Amazing Facts game of your own. Use facts from this book and your student book. You can write new facts, too. Write your questions in the squares. Write the correct answers on a separate piece of paper. Ask your teacher to check your game before you exchange games and play with friends.

(Supports Student Book D, page 106) **Creating a game; research; note-taking; socializing.** Encourage students to research answers they don't know. Store games in a box students can access during free time.

91

A. Write your ideas and thoughts about the unit theme, "Outdoor Adventures." What do you think the unit will be about? What kinds of outdoor activities do you enjoy doing with your friends? With your family? What environmental problems are you concerned about?

_____

_____

_____

_____

_____

_____

_____

_____

B. As you go through the unit, write your thoughts about each page. What would you like to find out more about? Use extra paper if you need more space.

_____

_____

_____

_____

_____

_____

_____

_____

_____

_____

(Supports Student Book D, page 107) **Home-School Connection; prewriting; predicting.** In Exercise A, students write their thoughts after participating in the class discussion of the unit opener page. Encourage students to come back to this page periodically to complete Exercise B. You may want to save a copy of this page in the student's **Assessment Portfolio**. Have students take this page home to share with their families.

C. Use the notes and ideas you wrote on page 92 to write about "Outdoor Adventures." What did you like most in the unit? Why? What did you like least? Why? What did you learn?

_____

_____

_____

_____

_____

_____

_____

_____

_____

_____

_____

_____

_____

_____

_____

_____

_____

_____

_____

_____

(Supports Student Book D, Theme 6. Use after page 126.) **Home-School Connection; writing opinions; using notes; recalling details; summarizing; self-assessment.** This page provides an opportunity for students to sum up their thoughts about the unit and to tell what they learned. You may want to save a copy of this page in the student's **Assessment Portfolio**. Have students take this page home to share with their families.

A. *Circle the letter of the best response.*

1. Something for you today?

    a. No, thanks.
    b. I'm just looking.
    c. I need a birthday present.

2. For a boy or a girl?

    a. For my uncle.
    b. I'd like a sweater.
    c. I wear medium.

3. How about this sweater?

    a. How much are they?
    b. How much is it?
    c. That's better.

4. It's twenty-five dollars.

    a. I'll try it on.
    b. I'll take it.
    c. I need it.

B. *Read carefully and complete the conversation.*

Can I help you?   *I'm looking for a sweater.*

What size do you take?   _____

Try this on.   _____

Try this one. It's smaller.   _____

It's fifty dollars.   _____

C. *Draw one person and describe what he or she is wearing.*

(Supports Student Book D, page 108) **Understanding sequence in conversations; describing clothing; reviewing colors.** Exercises A and B can be used for dialogue practice; in Exercise C, students can describe their pictures to a partner or to whole group.

PROBLEM SOLVING

A. *Sara and Jeff spent a week at Highland Mountain Camp with their classmates. The camp is open from February through July. The line graph shows how many students attended the camp last year. Look at the graph and answer the questions.*

1. About how many students went to the camp in April?
2. In which month did the fewest students go?
3. In which months did more than 200 students go?
4. In what two months did about the same number of students go?

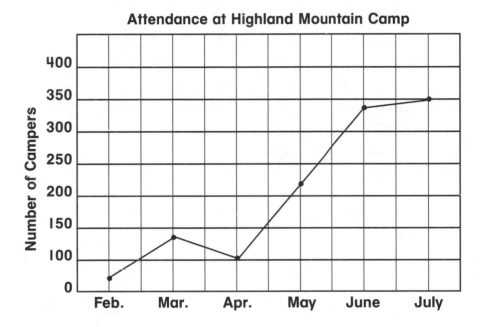

Attendance at Highland Mountain Camp

B. *Now make your own line graph. Use this data about the amount of snow that fell on Highland Mountain from January through April last year. Put the name of the graph at the top. What can you say about the monthly snowfalls?*

Highland Mountain Monthly Snowfalls	
Month	Amount of Snow (in inches)
January	34
February	51
March	42
April	10

(Supports Student Book D, page 109) **Solving problems logically; interpreting a graph; graphing; learning greater than/less than.** Have students work in pairs. For Exercise B, give each student graph paper and help them set up the graph, with the months at the bottom and *Amount of Snow* at the side.

A. *Periscopes are used on submarines. Read about early submarines, and then match the words on the left with their definitions on the right. Write the correct letter on the line. You may need to use a dictionary.*

The first submarine was called the **Marine Diver.** It was built in 1850 by a German inventor named Sebastian Bauer. During the **Diver**'s test dive, Bauer and his crew of two were trapped in the submarine for seven hours. The sub had sprung a leak and sunk in 50 feet (15 meters) of water. The only escape was through the hatch, but they couldn't open the hatch because the air pressure inside and outside the sub was not equalized. Finally, when the air pressure equalized, they opened the hatch and swam safely to the surface.

When he built his second submarine five years later, Bauer called it the **Marine Devil**. Four members of the **Devil**'s crew walked on a treadmill to power the sub. Other crew members took the world's first underwater photographs through the **Devil**'s windows. Bauer used the sub to experiment with an underwater sound-signaling system. He also worked on ways to purify the air in submarines.

1. marine _____   a. balanced

2. trapped _____   b. about the sea

3. hatch _____   c. to make a machine work

4. air pressure _____   d. a wheel with steps or a belt that moves

5. equalized _____   e. an opening in a ship's deck

6. power _____   f. to be unable to get out of a place

7. treadmill _____   g. to make clean

8. purify _____   h. the force of air on a surface

B. *Find out more about underwater photography. On a separate piece of paper, write three amazing facts about underwater photography.*

(Supports Student Book D, page 110) **Reading for a purpose; research; note-taking.** Correct Exercise A in class. Assign Exercise B as pair or group work. Direct students to appropriate reference materials. You may want to save this page in the student's **Assessment Portfolio.**

A. *Read the fable and answer the questions.*

The City Mouse and the Country Mouse

Once upon a time, the City Mouse went to visit his friend the Country Mouse. "My goodness," said the City Mouse when he arrived, "Your house is really small, and your furniture is very plain."

"Well, it suits me just fine, and I enjoy my quiet life here very much," replied the proud Country Mouse.

"What's for dinner?" asked the rude City Mouse.

"Well," said his friend, "I have some lovely country cheese and fresh country bread. And we can wash it all down with fresh milk.

"Humph!" exclaimed the City Mouse. "Don't you have anything more exciting to eat? Not even some raspberries, or maybe a kiwi or two?"

"Sorry, friend," sighed the Country Mouse, and he began to eat his dinner, but with less enjoyment than usual.

The next week, the Country Mouse went to visit the City Mouse. The City Mouse lived in a beautiful penthouse in a busy, exciting city. The City Mouse had prepared a banquet table that was filled end to end with all kinds of delicious food. The two friends were just beginning their meal when the neighbor's three cats came racing into the room. The terrified mice scampered to safety in the mouse hole. When the coast was clear, the Country Mouse headed for home. "I prefer my meals without entertainment," he said.

A crust of bread eaten in peace is better than a whole feast eaten in fear.

1. *Circle* **True** *or* **False:** The City Mouse liked the Country Mouse's house.

2. What did the Country Mouse offer his friend for dinner?

_____

3. What filled the City Mouse's banquet table end to end?

_____

4. *Circle* **True** *or* **False:** The two friends were frightened by three dogs.

5. What did the Country Mouse do at the end of the story?

6. Explain the "lesson" of the story, which is written in italics.

B. *On a separate piece of paper, write a short fable of your own. Give it a title, and be sure to include a "lesson." Illustrate it, if you want.*

(Supports Student Book D, page 111) **Reading for a purpose; creative writing; organizational planning.**
Students can complete Exercise A independently or in pairs. Accept long or short answers. Brainstorm ideas for Exercise B. Have students share their fables with class. You may want to save this page in the student's **Assessment Portfolio**.

A *Use a period(.), a comma (,), a questions mark (?), or an exclamation point (!) in the right places in these sentences.*

1. Stop A car is coming

2. What would you like for dinner

3. I hate candy soda and popcorn

4. Did you finish your homework yet

5. Last Saturday we went to the movies in the afternoon and then we went to visit some friends

6. Whose cat is that

7. Wow what a beautiful sunset

Use quotation marks (" ") in the right places in these sentences.

1. You shouldn't eat worms, said the doctor.

2. What's for dinner? asked Carlos.

3. Help! cried Superman.

4. Please clean up your room, said my mother.

Use an apostrophe (') in the right places in these sentences.

1. ★ My sisters boyfriend drives a sports car.
   ● So what?

2. ★ Where is your mothers office?
   ● In the same building as my fathers.

3. ★ Havent you ever seen *Beauty and the Beast*?
   ● No, I havent.

4. ★ Why dont you stay for lunch? Dont you like spaghetti?
   ● I love spaghetti, but I cant stay. Ill have lunch with you tomorrow.

(Supports Student Book D, page 112) **Punctuation.** Students work independently and correct in class. The first exercise teaches use of serial comma (number 3) and comma to separate clauses in a compound sentence (number 5). There may be more than one correct way to punctuate some sentences. Drill contractions and possessives, and teach plural possessives when class is ready.

Use periods, commas, question marks, exclamation points, apostrophes, and quotation marks in the right places in this story.

Captain Zero and her crew of fearless astronauts Lightspeed Starface and Milky Way were headed for a new galaxy They had already been in their spaceship for twenty-five years and they still had a long way to go to get to the new galaxy But even after twenty-five years the crews enthusiasm was high One day they were attacked by space pirates but they managed to get away from them Wow said Starface That was close What if those pirates had taken our fuel Then we wouldnt be able to get back to Earth What in the world would happen to us then asked Lightspeed You shouldnt worry so much said Milky Way Trust our good Captain Zero She knows what to do Just then Captain Zero came out of the captains quarters She looked mean and angry You astronauts she screamed You think Im **your** captain dont you But Im really the captain of the space pirates Youve had it And she laughed a horrible sickening disgusting ugly pirate laugh

(Supports Student Book D, pages 112-113) **Punctuation.** This exercise provides an opportunity to review punctuation marks. Review unfamiliar vocabulary before assigning exercise. There may be more than one way to punctuate some sentences.

99

A. *Look at page 114 of your student book. Complete the sentences about animal weather forecasters.*

1. A dog rolling on the ground is a _____

   _____ .

2. When a cat sneezes, _____

   _____ .

3. When dogs' tails straighten, _____

   _____ .

4. If you see sparks when you stroke a cat's back, _____

   _____ .

5. When dogs rub themselves in winter, _____

   _____ .

6. When an old cat acts like a frisky kitten, a _____

   _____ .

B. *Find more amazing facts about the weather. Number the facts and write them here. Use complete sentences.*

_____

_____

_____

_____

_____

_____

_____

_____

_____

(Supports Student Book D, page 114) **Reading for a purpose; research; note-taking.** You may want to have students work in small groups to research weather facts. Suggest appropriate reference materials. You may want to save this page in the student's **Assessment Portfolio**.

C. *Read the sentences carefully. Write* **True** *or* **False** *on the line after each one.*

1. The average person throws away more than three and a half pounds of trash every day. _____

2. Every month we throw away our own weight in packaging. _____

3. Most trash ends up in a landfill. _____

4. You can help cut down on the amount of trash in the world. _____

5. You can reuse old grocery bags. _____

6. Soda cans cannot be used again. _____

7. Paper in a landfill lasts 20-30 days. _____

8. Tin lasts 12-15 months. _____

9. Wood lasts forever. _____

10. Plastic lasts 5,000 years. _____

D. *Find out more about recycling. What kind of recycling program does your town or city have? What else could be done? How could more people be involved? Use extra paper if you need more space.*

_____

_____

_____

_____

_____

_____

_____

_____

(Supports Student Book D, pages 114-115) **Home-School Connection; reading for a purpose; using a variety of sources to get information.** Discuss answers to Exercise C in class. Exercise D can be a small-group or class project. Students can call or write to your town/city government for information. Discuss findings in class. You may want to save a copy of this page in the student's **Assessment Portfolio**. Have students take this page home to share with their families.

A Look at the pictures and answer the questions. Use complete sentences.

1. When did they wake up?

_____

_____

2. Where has your sister gone?

_____

_____

3. What did you grow in your garden?

_____

_____

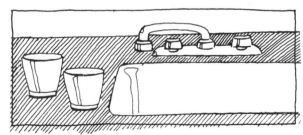

4. How much milk has she drunk already?

_____

_____

5. Where did he speak to Carmen?

_____

_____

(Supports Student Book D, pages 116-117) **Verb forms.** Students work independently to complete the exercise. Correct in class.

B Look at the example and answer the questions.

Example: Please drink your milk.

I have already drunk my milk. _____

1. Please eat your breakfast.

_____.

2. Please wake your sister up.

_____.

3. Please go to the library.

_____.

4. Please speak to Ali.

_____.

5. Please shake the crumbs off the napkins.

_____.

_____.

6. Please grow carrots in your garden.

_____.

_____.

Answer the questions about the story on student page 117.

1. What three things did Lou do when he woke up?

_____

2. What happened after he fell asleep again?

_____

3. What did Lou's mother do when she saw him still sleeping?

_____

4. What did Lou say after his mother told him to get ready for school?

_____

5. What did Lou's mother say to him after he had eaten his breakfast?

_____

6. What good reasons for going to school did Lou's mother give him?

_____

(Supports Student Book D, pages 116-117) **Past tense; present perfect tense; reading for a purpose.**
Correct in class. Remind students to change pronouns in numbers 1, 3, and 4 of the first exercise. In number
1, *your* becomes *my.* In number 2, *your* becomes *her.* In number 6, *your* becomes *my.*

103

Pollution has endangered many animals. Find out more about **endangered species.** *Choose one species and answer the questions about it. Use a separate piece of paper if you run out of space for writing here.*

Name of species_____

1. Where does the species live?

_____

_____

_____

2. Why is it endangered?

_____

_____

_____

_____

_____

3. What is being done to protect it?

_____

_____

_____

_____

_____

_____

_____

_____

_____

_____

(Supports Student Book D, page 118) **Research; note-taking; report writing.** Before assigning, be sure students understand *endangered species.* Suggested species: gray bat, Northern Right whale, California condor, Puerto Rican parrot. You may ask students to present their findings orally. You may want to save this page in the student's **Assessment Portfolio**.

Take a survey. Ask your friends and relatives what kinds of trash they recycle. After you have gathered your information, fill in the chart.

Recycling			
How Often	**Place**	**Items**	**Name**

(Supports Student Book D, page 119) **Home-School Connection; data collection; classifying; conducting a survey; comparing and contrasting.** Before assigning, suggest specifics for each category (e.g., under **Items:** paper, plastic, glass, tin/aluminum, toxic waste, etc.; under **Place:** dump, curbside, etc.) Discuss completed charts. You may want to save a copy of this page in the student's **Assessment Portfolio**. Have students take this page home to share with their families.

Balto the Brave: A True Story from Alaska

Put the sentences from "Balto the Brave" in the correct order.
Number them 1-16, and then copy them on a separate piece of
paper. The first one is done for you.

_____ Gunnar and Balto waited for the sled team from Golowin.

_____ The storm grew even worse.

_____ "We need the best men and the best sled dogs in the area."

_____ "You're a hero," the mayor said to Gunnar.

_____ People were sick with diphtheria.

_____ Gunnar and Balto didn't even slow down.

_____ "Balto is the smartest and bravest dog in all of Alaska."

_____ The medicine was still 400 frozen miles from Nome.

_____ The mayor of Nome radioed for help.

_____ In January of 1925, Nome, Alaska, was buried in snow.

_____ Just before dawn, the team reached Nome.

_____ "No, Balto is the hero," said Gunnar.

_1_ Balto was the lead dog on a team of sled dogs.

_____ The first sled driver reached the train.

_____ They needed medicine from the hospital in Anchorage.

_____ "We'll work in relay teams."

(Supports Student Book D, pages 120-123) **Identifying sequence in a story; understanding details in a story.** After students complete exercise independently, correct in class. If possible, show Nome, Alaska, on a map.

Balto the Brave: A True Story from Alaska

Write a new adventure for Balto and Gunnar. Include as many details as possible. Give your story a title, and illustrate it. Use more paper if your adventure grows too big for the space here.

_____

_____

_____

_____

_____

_____

_____

_____

(Supports Student Book D, pages 120-123) **Creative writing; organizational planning.** Have students share stories with class. Post completed stories and artwork on class bulletin board. You may want to save this page in the student's **Assessment Portfolio**.

The Mole and the Water Rat

Use the words in the Data Bank. Finish the paragraphs about the Mole and the Water Rat.

The Mole was working hard. It was _____, and he was spring-cleaning his underground house. His _____ ached, and his arms were tired. He could feel the sunshine _____ the fresh air calling to him. _____ he stopped cleaning. He climbed up, up, up, and popped out of the _____ into the sunlight.

He _____ the fields and came out onto the bank of a river. He had _____ seen a river before. He sat _____ on the grassy bank and listened to the water. Then he _____ something on the opposite bank. _____ was a small face—a little brown face with whiskers. It was the Water Rat. "Hello, Mole," said the Water Rat in a _____ voice. "Would you like to come over?"

The _____ didn't know the ways of the river. "How can I get to you?" he _____. The Rat rowed across in a little _____ and white boat. The Mole stepped timidly in. The two animals _____ friends at once.

DATA BANK

ground	became	friendly
saw	back	Mole
spring	and	blue
Suddenly	down	never
asked	It	crossed

(Supports Student Book D, page 124) **Reading comprehension; cloze exercise; syntax.** Students read sentences from the story they listened to on student book page 124. This exercise provides an opportunity for students to review the story and to learn syntax. Correct in class. You may want to save this page in the student's **Assessment Portfolio**.

© Addison-Wesley Publishing Company

Make an Amazing Facts game of your own. Use facts from this book and your student book. You can write new facts, too. Write your questions in the squares. Write the correct answers on a separate piece of paper. Ask your teacher to check your game before you exchange games and play with friends.

(Supports Student Book D, page 126) **Creating a game; research; note-taking; socializing.** Encourage students to research answers they don't know. Store games in a box students can access during free time.